Supercharge Your Project Management Career™

A Step-by-Step Self-Assessment, Workbook, and Guide to Landing Your Dream Project Management Job

NATALIE BERKIW-SCENNA, PMP

Table of Contents

Introduction to Supercharge Your Project Management Career

Project management is one of the most exciting careers!

It's an expanding field of expertise across every industry, and it presents us with limitless opportunities.

But, how do we compete in an ever-growing competitive space? Let me ask you this: How are you setting yourself apart from your competition?

This guide and workbook called **Supercharge Your Project Management Career** is going to help you answer this important question. In fact, this book is completely unique because we're not going to be covering project management methodology. There are hundreds of books that already do that. Instead, we're going to focus on how you can take your project management career to the **next level**.

My name is Natalie Berkiw-Scenna, and I've been in project management for well over 20 years and PMP certified since 2009. I bring a wealth of experience as someone who's spent time on both sides of the hiring table. I've worked hard to climb the Project Management career ladder myself, and I've interviewed, hired, and onboarded countless project managers over the years. In addition to this, I've been coaching and supporting others who are interested in entering this field with skill-building exercises, resume-writing, and relationship-building to help project managers like you get ahead.

Whether you're a seasoned project manager, or you're just starting out in your project management career, I invite you to join me as we **walk through several actionable steps** to building your confidence, credibility, and presence in order to supercharge your project management career.

This **workbook is comprehensive** and it will require you to be *hands-on*. Let's walk through these specific, actionable steps that you can use to stand out and shine.

Your possibilities are limitless. Now, it's time for you to get noticed.

Identifying Your Personal Core Values

In the initial section of this guide and workbook, we're going to start by completing a **personal self-assessment**. I want you to develop a great understanding of *who* you are, *what* is important you, and allow you to create your own **definition of personal success**.

Let's start with the first step in your personal assessment around identifying your **personal core values**. These are your beliefs and traits that guide your behaviors and decision-making.

Our core values identify who we are, what we stand for, and they can impact our personal relationships.

Your core values are unique to you and there's no right or wrong answer. Use this personal assessment to better understand who you are and what's important to you.

Let's review a list of core values on the next page, and I invite you to select your **top 5 values**.

Supercharge Your Project Management Career
Core Values Worksheet

Review the list of core values and check off your top 5 personal values.

☐ Abundance	☐ Faith	☐ Kindness
☐ Acceptance	☐ Finances	☐ Loyalty
☐ Advancement	☐ Freedom	☐ Order
☐ Adventure	☐ Generosity	☐ Power
☐ Affection	☐ Gratitude	☐ Prosperity
☐ Authenticity	☐ Happiness	☐ Relationships
☐ Balance	☐ Harmony	☐ Religion
☐ Compassion	☐ Honesty	☐ Respect
☐ Connection	☐ Humanity	☐ Status
☐ Cooperation	☐ Invention	☐ Success
☐ Courage	☐ Innovation	☐ Trustworthiness
☐ Excitement	☐ Integrity	☐ Wealth
☐ Endurance	☐ Intelligence	☐ Wellness

Identifying Your Personal Motivators

Now that you've had a chance to identify the core values that are most important to you, we're going to start exploring our **personal motivators**. I want you think about what motivates you. We are all motivated differently and driven by either internal or external forces. Our personal motivators give us purpose, meaning, and the drive to succeed with everything that we do.

Similar to how your core values are unique to you, your list of what motivates you is also completely unique and unlike anyone else. This is all part of gaining a better understanding of who you are, and it will help you define what's important as you look to grow your project management career.

Let's take a look at a list of key motivators in the worksheet on the next page. Take a few minutes to **select your top 5 motivators** that resonate most with you. Again, there is no right or wrong answer, but this will help you gain a better understanding of what's important to you.

What did you come up with? What insight does this give you about what motivates you? And how can you leverage this when you're thinking about your next career move?

 I can tell you that my personal motivators include Learning, Excelling, Creativity, Challenge and Excitement which tells me that I thrive in an environment where I can be constantly challenged and there's always opportunities to learn new knowledge and skills.
- *Natalie Berkiw-Scenna, PMP*

Supercharge Your Project Management Career
Personal Motivators Worksheet

Review the 23 types of personal motivators, and check off the top 5 that you feel are most important to you.

☐ Autonomy (self-directed)

☐ Impact

☐ Social Responsibility

☐ Challenge

☐ Learning

☐ Teamwork

☐ Creativity

☐ Money

☐ Variety

☐ Developing Others

☐ Ownership

☐ Empathy

☐ Pressure

☐ Excelling

☐ Prestige

☐ Excitement

☐ Problem Solving

☐ Family

☐ Purpose

☐ Friendship

☐ Recognition

☐ Fun

☐ Service

Source: The Culture Works: The Motivators Assessment

Defining Your Ideal Work Environment

Alright, now that we've had the opportunity to identify what you value most with your core values, and what motivates you with your personal motivators, next let's think about your **ideal work environment**. This is another important step in your personal self-assessment. As you think about your next career move, you can focus your efforts on job opportunities that provide you with the ideal work environment for you.

Review the Ideal Work Environment worksheet on the next page. Then, I invite you to check off as many items as you'd like but try to be as specific as possible.

Consider options such as working indoors vs. outdoors, working for a large organization vs a small company, in-office vs remote work, etc.

As you will see, there are a **wide variety of options** when it comes to your work environment. Take a moment and think about what might work the best for you and your preferred lifestyle.

Supercharge Your Project Management Career
Ideal Work Environment Worksheet

Think about the work environment that you most highly value. Check the boxes of the working conditions that you would prefer.

☐ Indoors ☐ Outdoors

☐ Relaxed and Casual ☐ Formal

☐ Large organization ☐ Medium company ☐ Small company

☐ Brand new start-up ☐ Mature organization with established reputation

☐ Relaxed and calm-paced ☐ Fast-paced

☐ Flexible work hours ☐ Set working schedule

☐ Independent ☐ Franchised

☐ Long commute ☐ Short commute ☐ Remote / work from home

☐ Requires business travel ☐ Doesn't require business travel

☐ Established training and development programs ☐ Commitment to excellence ☐ Access to amenities (cafes, private work areas, on-site gyms.)

☐ Room for advancement opportunities ☐ Respect for diversity ☐ Competitive compensation and benefits package

☐ Strong employee recognition programs ☐ Great workplace culture ☐ Other: _____ _____

Identifying Your Goals and Defining Personal Success

Alright, so far you've defined your core values, your personal motivators, and your ideal work environment. Next, let's think about the important question of what does success look like for you? Let's set some clear goals to help you define where you want to be in the future.

Success looks completely different for everyone, and again, your definition will be unique to you.

But before we jump in, let me start off with some great news!

The **demand for project managers is extremely high** and it continues to grow every year. The reality is that there are plenty of opportunities for career advancement for project managers *across nearly every industry*.

What industry are you currently in? What industry are you hoping to get into? Do you see yourself remaining in the same industry as you look at career advancement opportunities or would you like to cross over into a completely new area?

Project managers can be found in almost every industry. Here are a few examples of industries just to give you an understanding of the wide variety of options that are available to us:

> Healthcare, finance, automotive, legal, manufacturing, transportation, construction, research, energy, information technology (IT), aerospace, communications, etc.

What industry is of most interest to you when you think about your future?

Next, I want you to answer some important questions on the next page to help you determine your personal goals, followed by a second worksheet that will allow you to develop your own **personal goals statement** based on the activities you've completed so far.

Supercharge Your Project Management Career
Definition of Success Worksheet

Answer these questions to help you define your personal career goals.

When you think about your project management career, where do you want to be in 1 year? How about 3-5 years?

Are you looking for an entry role in project management? Or a promotion to a more senior role? Or a lateral move to gain different experiences?

What are you hoping to achieve? More income? Greater benefits? More challenging projects? Better work/life balance? What's important to you?

What does success mean to you? What would success look like? How would you know that you've achieved it?

Supercharge Your Project Management Career
Career Goals Statement Worksheet

Using the great information you have learned about yourself in the last few chapters, start to fill in the following career goals statement for yourself.

As a project manager that values

(Add your core values here)

that is motivated by

(Add your personal motivators here)

my goal is to take my project management career to the next level in the

(Add your desired industry here)

where I can work in an environment that includes

(Add your ideal environment features here)

and I know I'll be successful when

(Add your personal definition of success here)

Defining Your Key Skills and Strengths

In this chapter, let's spend some time focusing on your key skills and strengths. These are the specific skills that you personally excel in and they set you apart or *differentiate* you from your project management competition.

There are many skills that every project manager should have in order to be successful in their role. They can be broken down into two types of skills.

First, we have **technical skills**. These are often referred to as "hard" skills and related to project planning and execution. These can include the ability to write project charters and detailed reports, develop the project scope, time and budget, scheduling, risk mitigation, data collection, and so on. Most project managers have at least some level of proficiency in these skills, and they will naturally strengthen with time and experience.

The second type of skills are **interpersonal skills**. These are often referred to as soft skills, but there is nothing actually soft about them. In fact, these are often the skills that help set us apart. Strong interpersonal skills are in very high demand, and they are critical for you to have and develop as a project manager. A few examples of these include leadership, communication, decision-making, time management, active listening, emotional intelligence, public speaking, and negotiation.

Now, we're going to look at a detailed list of technical and interpersonal skills on the following two pages. As you review the worksheets, think about which skills you excel in. This list will consist of both hard skills and soft skills.

But here's my challenge to you. I want you to **select a maximum of 10** skills. You may feel that you are good at more of the skills on the list, but I want you to think about what you're really strong in. By restricting it to no more than 10, it will help you focus on your key strengths. So go ahead and review the worksheets on the next two pages, and check the boxes of those key skills now.

Supercharge Your Project Management Career
Personal Skills Assessment Worksheet

Review the list of technical and interpersonal skills and check your top 10 skills.

☐ Developing project charters	☐ Project execution	☐ Conflict management
☐ Stakeholder analysis	☐ Report writing	☐ Motivating others
☐ Work breakdown structures	☐ Project plan development	☐ Active Listening
☐ Developing communications plans	☐ Critical thinking	☐ Resilience
☐ Identifying and managing risks	☐ Creative thinking	☐ Flexibility
☐ Performance reporting	☐ Inspiring Others	☐ Written communications
☐ Capturing lessons learned	☐ Problem solving	☐ Verbal communications
☐ Performance reporting	☐ Financial modeling	☐ Non-verbal communications
☐ Budgeting	☐ Project lifecycle management	☐ Presentation development
☐ Strategic planning	☐ Mind mapping	☐ Accountability
☐ Organizing	☐ Logical reasoning	☐ Emotional intelligence
☐ Managing people	☐ Team building	☐ Presentation development
☐ Project scope development	☐ Political and cultural awareness	☐ Versatility

12

Supercharge Your Project Management Career
Personal Skills Assessment Worksheet

Review the list of technical and interpersonal skills and check your top 10 skills.

☐ Facilitation	☐ Educating	☐ Public speaking
☐ Negotiation	☐ Allocating resources	☐ Data analysis
☐ Conflict resolution	☐ Goal setting	☐ Brainstorming
☐ Leadership	☐ Scheduling	☐ Design
☐ Persuasion	☐ Prioritization	☐ Innovating
☐ Influencing	☐ Planning and forecasting	☐ Other: _____ _____
☐ Coaching and mentoring	☐ Task planning	☐ Other: _____ _____
☐ Time management	☐ Task tracking	☐ Other: _____ _____
☐ Decision making	☐ Streamlining	☐ Other: _____ _____
☐ Relationship building	☐ Collaboration	☐ Other: _____ _____
☐ Multi-tasking	☐ Mediation	☐ Other: _____ _____
☐ Meeting management	☐ Presenting	☐ Other: _____ _____
☐ Empowering others	☐ Networking	☐ Other: _____ _____

Exploring Your Skills That Others Identify, and Defining Your Superpowers

Now that you've had the chance to complete a personal skills assessment, I want you to start exploring what **others feel are your strengths**. Sometimes those around you see skills and strengths that we don't even realize we have.

Let's start to think about what makes you stand out to others. Think about your team and colleagues, your boss, your fellow students, your friends, and your family. What do you think they would say are your strengths?

Here is an exercise for you. And you can take this as far as you'd like. Explore what others have to say. You can do this in a few ways, and if you're feeling ambitious, you can do them all. Use the Skills and Strengths Identified By Others Worksheet on the next page using the following exercises:

Select a few colleagues, friends, or family members and ask them to provide you with some feedback. Ask them "What do you think are my greatest skills and strengths?" and/or "What do you think I'm really good at?" Write down what they say on the next page.

Think about your last performance review at work. What did your boss say about you? What did they point out as your best skills? Better yet, do you have access to your last review? If so, go back to it and write down in your worksheet what skills they highlighted.

If you're feeling even more ambitious, I'll invite you to take this to social media. Ask your wider social network about what they see as your top strengths. Record this in your worksheet.

This is a great way to learn what skills and strengths you have.

Once you have completed this exercise, do a side-by-side comparison with your own list in the worksheet. Are there any surprises? Your list might be longer than 10 now. These are the things that make you shine!

Next, think about your **super skills** or **"superpowers"** by narrowing this list down to the skills you are absolutely the best in. Select the **top 3** from this combined list. Ask yourself what are you really good at, and what skills are you hyperspecialized in? This is what *differentiates you from other project managers* and makes you unique.

Write down these top 3 superpowers in your worksheet. You can then revisit these again when we start using story-telling to build your resume.

Skills and Strengths Identified by Others, and Your "Superpowers" Worksheet

Ask others for feedback on what they feel are your skills and strengths. Then compare this list with your top 10 skills. Next, select your top 3 super-strengths.

Ask others what they feel are your skills and strengths and list them here.

Compare the list above with the skills and strengths from your list. Which ones overlap on both lists?

Select the top three skills you feel are your strongest based on your own assessment, and from feedback from others. What are your 3 super strengths (or "superpowers")?:

Developing Your Personal Portfolio of Praise, and Building Self-Confidence

In this chapter we're going to work on building up your confidence level and developing you as a personal brand. But before we do this, let's start with what this means. What is a **personal brand**?

We often think of branding when we think of physical objects and company names, and how those objects make us feel. Branding can make us feel a sense of luxury, or dependability for example. But in this case, the brand is **you**. It's all about how others see you and how you make them feel. Do they feel that they can count on you? Do they see you as an expert? You have to remember that everything you do contributes to your personal brand.

This can include how you treat the people around you, how others perceive your strengths and weaknesses, how they see you react under pressure, how you communicate, what you post on social media, etc. You have the ability to **control your own personal brand**.

This is all about managing your reputation, and it's up to you to make sure you're the one that's managing and mastering your message to the world.

But before we look at building your personal brand, let's discuss how we can **build your confidence level**. Self-confidence is essential when you're looking at taking your project management career to the next level. You need to understand the value that you bring to the table, and believe in yourself and your own abilities in order for others to believe in them too. The greater your confidence level, the more risks you're willing to take to make tangible improvements in your life, which ultimately leads to greater rewards. So, if there is a dream project management job that you're seeking, self-confidence will be what encourages you to go after that dream.

Developing Your Personal Portfolio of Praise™, and Building Self-Confidence

Let's review how you can do this. Start off with what you know about how others see you and your strengths. I want you to begin to develop your own **Personal Portfolio of Praise**™. This is what I call the collection of compliments and positive feedback that you have received over the years.

Have you ever been sent a nice email from your boss, a colleague or maybe even your teacher to tell you that you did a great job? Maybe it was related to a project you completed, or a presentation that you created. Or maybe someone verbally said something positive – like "Hey, that was a great meeting you led" or "Thanks for the comprehensive email you sent" or "Good job on that project!"

This exercise is for you to start collecting those **great comments and feedback**, and begin placing them in one central location so that you can access them at any time. And if you get verbal feedback such as a compliment or a thank you for a job well done, make sure you take the time to document it, and record who said it and when it happened. I encourage you to start doing this going forward.

Next, I want you to go back to any of your past annual performance reviews and pick out all of the positive aspects from this process, and then document this in your Personal Portfolio of Praise™ on the next page.

This growing list of feedback will be great to pull out if you ever have days when your confidence level feels low. Seeing the positive feedback from those around you will always help perk you back up, and give you the confidence boost you need.

Supercharge Your Project Management Career
"Personal Portfolio of Praise" Worksheet

Use this worksheet to list out your collection of any compliments and positive feedback that you've ever received. You can pull this from past emails, performance reviews, social media posts, verbal feedback, etc. Document what was said, and by whom.

Identifying Your List of Key Accomplishments and Achievements

Let's continue to build on your level of confidence. One of the best ways we can do this is to create a list of everything you've accomplished that you are most proud of.

When you think about your career so far, what would you say are your **greatest accomplishments and achievements**?

If you are a seasoned project manager, you likely have a long list of projects already completed under your belt. Consider any courses that you took that broadened your knowledge or skill sets, and any designations like your PMP or CAPM that you achieved or are actively working on. Maybe it's the great relationships you have built.

If you're new to the work world, just finishing up school, and looking for your first, entry level project management role, you should still have plenty of experiences to draw from. It can be a list of your school projects, collaborations with your fellow students, a really great class you took that you passed with flying colors, or perhaps a volunteer opportunity you were involved with.

It's important to know that your list of accomplishments will be completely unique to you. No one else will have had the same set of experiences and achievements that you have. This is important to understand as we look to set you apart from your competition.

Start to list your accomplishments and achievements in the worksheet on the next page. This will be used in a future chapter when we start developing your resume and identifying how you can set yourself apart from your competition.

Supercharge Your Project Management Career
Accomplishments and Achievements Worksheet

Create a list of all your accomplishments and achievements that you are proud of including projects completed, education, designations, skills you developed, relationships you built, awards you won, significant tasks you completed, etc.

Defining Your Personal Brand

Let's focus specifically on what you can do to start building your personal brand. I mentioned earlier that this is all about *how* others see you and *how* you make them feel. Everything you do contributes to your personal brand.

I want you to begin thinking about what you want your personal brand to be. Start by asking yourself a few questions and answering them in the Personal Brand worksheet on the next page. Take some time to think about **how you want others to see you**.

Once you've defined what you want this to be, then we'll start looking at how you can master your message, your reputation, and ultimately your personal brand.

Personal Branding Worksheet

Use this section to start thinking about what you want your personal brand to be. This is all about how others think and feel about you.

What do you want to
be known for?

How do you want
to stand out from
your competition?

How do you want
others to feel
when they think
about you?

How would you want
others to describe
you?

How are you currently
putting yourself out
there in the world?
Think about how you
communicate, social
media presence, etc.

Mastering Your Personal Brand Message

When you're thinking about supercharging your project management career, you **don't want to be seen in the same light** as every other project manager competing against you for the same job opportunities.

You want to develop your own, unique, and authentic personal brand that sets you apart from the rest of the competition. In the last worksheet, you brainstormed what you would like your personal brand to be.

Now let's talk about how you can **master your message** with everyone around you so that they begin to see you in the same light. Let's jump into a number of actionable steps that you can do to show the world who you are, and control your personal branding message.

Let's start with some *easy, quick wins*.

1) When was the last time you updated your email signature line?

This is an easy way to add a professional touch to your emails. And not just for your work email. Do you have a professional-looking email signature line for your personal email as well? Email is still one of the most common forms of communication today in the work environment, and you have an opportunity to jazz it up and make it your own.

Consider adding a headshot photo, designing something with color or adding your company logo or an image to make it more unique and memorable. You can even add a favorite quote or a statement about who you are and what's important to you. Your signature line should uniquely reflect who you are as a project management professional. Consider a free, online resource such as Canva.com to design a memorable email signature that matches your personal brand.

Mastering Your Personal Brand Message

2. Explore how you currently use social media, and what types of information you post.

Since social media is very public, you need to remember that any potential employer can easily access this information and begin to formulate their own thoughts and feelings about who you are. The question I have for you is this - will it match the same thoughts and feelings that you are aiming to achieve with your intended personal brand?

Consider completing an audit of your current social media channels, and if it makes sense, identify any information, posts or photos you might want to consider keeping private.

3. Think about how you're showing up and demonstrating yourself as an expert in project management?

If you really want to develop yourself as a personal brand, you need to be able to communicate that you are an expert to those within your social networks, and beyond to the whole world. You have a unique voice, and an opportunity to truly master your message by putting yourself out there and demonstrating your knowledge and skill sets.

So, how can you do this? Consider this question: Are you a **consumer of knowledge** or a **producer of knowledge**? A consumer of knowledge gathers information from others and reads websites, articles, books, blogs, etc. that are written by others. On the other hand, a producer of knowledge is someone who creates these assets for others to benefit from, and to demonstrate their experience and expertise.

If you want to truly master your personal branding message, you need to find a good balance of both. By being a producer of knowledge, this quickly demonstrates to others that you're confident in your knowledge and skills. This goes a long way to showing that you're an expert in project management and in your industry.

Mastering Your Personal Brand Message

This list shows some examples of what you can do to be a producer of knowledge, and to demonstrate that you are an expert in the eyes of potential employers. Consider if any of these make sense to you, and what you're most comfortable with.

Start a project management blog and advertise it to your social networks. Write about your personal project experiences and lessons learned.

Apply to be a speaker at a local project management event, and talk about one of your projects, how you set it up, and your lessons learned. Consider partnering with a colleague if that makes you feel more comfortable to present.

Post regularly on social media about project management. LinkedIn is the ideal place for professional posts, and we'll talk about this platform shortly.

Write an eBook on what your most knowledgeable about, and go ahead and publish it on Amazon.

Create a website dedicated to your project portfolio and all your successes.

Start a podcast about project management. You need minimal equipment to get started and can do this with just your phone.

Write an article and submit it to a project management magazine.

Submit one of your projects for a project competition. You can see if there are any in your area. Check your local chapter of the Project Management Institute.

Start a YouTube Channel and talk about anything related to project management.

Share other people's content. Find a great article or book? Share it and comment about how you found this to be helpful to you.

We touched on a number of ways that you can show up, gain incredible visibility and demonstrate yourself as an authority and expert in the project management space. Did any of those opportunities sound interesting to you? Consider how you can start **mastering your message** and **building your personal brand**.

Developing Your LinkedIn Profile

LinkedIn is a **social media platform** that is specifically geared towards connecting with other professionals and provides an ideal environment for you to set yourself up as an expert in project management.

Are you currently on LinkedIn, and if so, are you actively engaging on this platform? If not, you absolutely should be. Your LinkedIn presence should be an **extension of your personal brand**.

Make sure you have a great headshot that shows who you are without a distracting background. Consider using a professional photographer to get your headshots done, or ask a friend or family member to take a photo of you from the shoulders up with a solid background behind you. Make sure you have good lighting without a lot of shadows on your face. I often see LinkedIn profiles that are missing a photo, which makes their profile feel less personal and they miss a great opportunity for others to feel connected.

If you want to portray your personal brand, make sure you have a professional image that matches that message.

Secondly, leverage the **About Me** section and tell the story of who you are and what's important to you. This section doesn't need to read like a resume. This is your opportunity to be creative, and to talk about what your passionate about and what sets you apart. Consider all the great information you've collected so far in this course like your core values, your list of greatest accomplishments, your superpowers, etc. Use your unique voice to share who you are in this section and add any elements that you want to highlight. Since LinkedIn is searchable by hiring managers and headhunters, make sure your About Me section is filled with **keywords** including "project management" and all the skills you identified during your self-assessment.

Remember that LinkedIn is your **personal and professional billboard** that costs you nothing but your time to create.

Create your About Me section on the next page and use this to develop or enhance your profile on LinkedIn.

Supercharge Your Project Management Career
LinkedIn "About Me" Worksheet

LinkedIn should be an extension of your personal brand. Develop the "About Me" section to tell the story of who you are and what's important to you. Be creative, talk about what you're passionate about, and describe what sets you apart.

Leverage all the great information you developed in this workbook so far.

Developing Your LinkedIn Profile

Other ways to easily improve your LinkedIn Profile is to develop a **headline** that provides a brief summary of who you are, what your passionate about, or what value you bring. This is the first line that other LinkedIn users will see on your profile. Make sure you take a few minutes to customize this to set yourself apart from others. This is your opportunity to be creative.

To edit your headline, click the edit icon at the top of your profile (demonstrated by a little pencil icon). This is the section you fill out with your name, headline, current position, industry, location, etc.

Here is my personal LinkedIn page as an example:

You can also personalize the **cover photo** at the top to truly stand out. LinkedIn already offers you a number of options to select from, or you can create something that is truly unique. Free online resources like Canva allow you to easily create a LinkedIn cover image from an existing template or from scratch.

Networking and Building Relationships

In this chapter, we are going to talk about networking and building relationships with **like-minded professionals** in your field.

These activities are incredibly important in terms of giving you visibility to get you noticed, opening doors to new opportunities, allowing you to grow your status with others, boosting your self-confidence, and developing long-lasting relationships that will help you get ahead.

How are you currently networking with others? Have you already developed a number of great relationships where you currently work? How about at different companies within your industry? And do you keep in touch periodically with past colleagues, acquaintances, or past teachers and fellow students?

Always be mindful about your interactions with others and actively work to build relationships based on trust with those around you. One thing you can do is when you say you're going to do or finish something by a specific time, hold yourself accountable to follow through. Keeping your word can feel surprisingly rare these days and it's a great way to build trust.

Also, have you ever considered getting a **mentor**? A mentor is someone who provides guidance, motivation, emotional support, and role modeling. This might be a leader in your organization or someone else in your industry that you want to learn from. Consider setting up time with someone who you admire and begin nurturing that relationship. Once you have a good rapport, ask if they would be willing to meet with you periodically in a mentorship capacity. You'll find that most people are flattered when asked and are happy to help someone navigate their career path.

In the last chapter, we talked about setting up your LinkedIn account. Many interactions today are online, and LinkedIn is the best central place to connect with other like-minded professionals in both the project management space, as well as your specific industry.

Networking and Building Relationships

On LinkedIn, start following companies and influential people that you're interested in, and explore groups with similar interests. See what information they share, and take the time to engage in their content. Take a moment to like a post that captures your interest, and add a thoughtful comment about how the information they shared resonated with you.

One thing you can do to start building relationships is to invite others to connect. But here's the catch, take the time to include a quick message about why you're requesting their connection on LinkedIn. For example, mention that you saw one of their posts and are interested in their content and would like to follow them, or that you seem to share an interest in the same industry and that you're looking to connect with like-minded professionals. Regardless, don't send an empty request. Take a few minutes to make a meaningful connection. They are more likely to accept and respond with a message back, and then you can decide if you want to keep the conversation going.

The same concept goes if someone sends you a request on LinkedIn to connect. Even if they don't immediately send a message, accept the invitation and then send them a quick thank you message for connecting.

Remember when we touched on whether you want to be a consumer or a producer of knowledge? LinkedIn is a great place to see what's happening in your industry and to gain access to posts, articles, webinars, etc. If you find a great article, share it with your network and consider tagging the author. And if you decide to become a **producer of knowledge** by writing project management articles, blogs, videos, etc., leverage LinkedIn to share this information. Others will start to see you as a project management expert and begin following you. If you regularly post content, you'll be surprised at how quickly your network and number of connections begin to grow.

LinkedIn is also a great hub to connect with others around job opportunities. Keep your eyes open for job postings, and begin developing key relationships. This starts with building a presence here online.

Building Your Resume Through Storytelling

The focus of the next few chapters will be around building your resume in order to position yourself for the project management role you want. We're going to talk about how to leverage the art of story-telling to make your skills and abilities jump off the page. Let's work together on making you **stand out from your competition**.

The reality is this, we all make up an incredibly talented and skilled group of professionals. We're given the challenging task of taking on complex projects, breaking them down into manageable tasks and activities, and leading diverse groups through to project completion. So, how does someone reviewing these project management resumes select the top contenders to interview?

As project managers, we have the good fortune of being highly analytical and task-oriented, and these skills serve us well when we are managing and leading our projects. However, we need to start thinking differently when we're looking to develop a great resume that truly showcases who we are, what our personal brand is, and what unique skills we bring to the table. This is where **storytelling** comes into play.

This is because if your resume ends up being a simple, bulleted list of all the tasks you've completed, then you're not offering any insights into the value you bring and your resume is going to look exactly like the rest of the resume pile. Resumes that apply storytelling allow the resume reader to immediately **visualize the value** that this project manager brings. That applicant figuratively jumps off the page, and like a good story, the reader wants to learn more.

Project management positions can be very competitive. When a hiring manager is inundated with handfuls of resumes, it can be very challenging for the reviewer when all the resumes look the same as each other. My goal for you is to **create a resume that clearly stands out.**

Building Your Resume Through Storytelling

Storytelling is the art of using words to create an *experience* for the reader's imagination. It evokes emotion. And as humans, we all love a good story. In fact, we crave it, and it makes us feel connected to others.

Have you ever read a really good book where the author did a great job of describing the main character and you immediately connected with the storyline? In fact, you probably couldn't stop turning the pages because you wanted to learn more about what happens next.

Well, in this case, you're both the *author* and the *main character*. It's up to you to **bring your character to life** so that you entice the reader (the resume reviewer) to want to learn more about you. Like any good story, you need a character (you), a conflict or challenge (your projects and initiatives), and a resolution (the outcome and the *value*). Your goal should be for the person reviewing the resume to say, "Wow, this looks like a great candidate. I have to bring this person in for an interview to learn about *how* they did that."

Let's dig into how you can apply storytelling so that your resume immediately gets noticed.

Resume Examples and Storytelling Formula

When applying storytelling to your resume, this is all about showcasing the value that you bring that **sets you apart**. You can apply storytelling in your resume with a simple formula:

Leading Word + Accomplishment + Value

Start with a great leading word, describe what you accomplished (or a challenge you overcame), and then describe the value of that accomplishment.

Let me give you a few real examples that highlight the differences between resume content without and with storytelling.
Here are two examples of task-oriented items I see on many resumes, **without storytelling**:

- "Developed a governance model for this project."
- "Collected project and process data and presented it to key stakeholders."

Now, here are a few similar examples **with storytelling** applied:

- "Championed the development and implementation of a new governance model and department leadership structure that included the consolidation of several programs which resulted in improved advocacy efforts for fundraising, elevated the promotion of the overall brand, and supported greater decision-making."
- "Aligned and positioned the data collection of our call center improvement project with our organization's key metrics and KPIs, and clearly demonstrated how our implementation directly transformed the overall satisfaction of our customers and led to both increased revenue per client and greater customer retention."

Can you *feel* the difference? By leveraging the art of storytelling, you allow your accomplishments to instantly catch the attention of the reviewer. Explore writing storytelling statements for your resume. Be the **superhero** in your resume story.

Supercharge Your Project Management Career
Resume Storytelling Worksheet

Review the list of great leading words below and then begin creating your resume storytelling statements that include a Leading Word + Accomplishment + Value on the next few pages.

Resume Leading Words

Accelerated	Improved
Achieved	Launched
Aligned	Led
Built	Leveraged
Championed	Managed
Created	Navigated
Cultivated	Piloted
Defined	Positioned
Delivered	Prioritized
Designed	Provided
Developed	Resolved
Directed	Secured
Engaged	Spearheaded
Elevated	Steered
Executed	Streamlined
Facilitated	Surpassed
Implemented	Transformed
Influenced	Upgraded
Initiated	Validated

Supercharge Your Project Management Career
Resume Storytelling Worksheet

Begin creating your resume storytelling statements that include a Leading Word + Accomplishment + Value.

LEADING WORD +
ACCOMPLISHMENT
+ VALUE

LEADING WORD +
ACCOMPLISHMENT
+ VALUE

LEADING WORD +
ACCOMPLISHMENT
+ VALUE

LEADING WORD +
ACCOMPLISHMENT
+ VALUE

LEADING WORD +
ACCOMPLISHMENT
+ VALUE

Supercharge Your Project Management Career
Resume Storytelling Worksheet

Begin creating your resume storytelling statements that include a Leading Word + Accomplishment + Value.

LEADING WORD +
ACCOMPLISHMENT
+ VALUE

LEADING WORD +
ACCOMPLISHMENT
+ VALUE

LEADING WORD +
ACCOMPLISHMENT
+ VALUE

LEADING WORD +
ACCOMPLISHMENT
+ VALUE

LEADING WORD +
ACCOMPLISHMENT
+ VALUE

Additional Resume Tips and Applying for Project Manager Jobs

Consider all the information you've collected about yourself. You completed a self-assessment to determine your core values, your key motivators, your ideal work environment, your skills and superpowers, your Personal Portfolio of Praise, and all of your accomplishments and achievements. Now you have the perfect opportunity to start weaving all of these valuable pieces of information into your resume to truly set yourself apart. These attributes are completely unique to you. Leverage the storytelling formula to highlight what sets you apart from your competition so that **your resume stands out from the crowd**.

Now, when you're preparing to apply for a position, you'll also want to accompany your resume with a great cover letter. This provide an additional opportunity to tell the story of who you are, why you're passionate about what you do, and how you're the perfect candidate for the position. Again, you have a ton of great material to work with now.

Remember your personal brand? Your cover letter should reflect how you want others to see you. **Be the expert.** If you decided to start a blog, podcast, website, published article, eBook, etc., make sure you highlight this in your cover letter and where they can go to learn more. **Give them the chance to see you shine**.

Make sure you're using a font that is legible and easy to read for your resume. Some examples of fonts that are ideal for resumes include Arial, Georgia, Helvetica, Tahoma, Times New Roman, or Verdana. Take advantage of **bolding** and *italics* when you want to direct attention to any specific attributes within both your cover letter and your resume.

Now, another tip that I want to stress is to never write a blanket statement on your resume that you have "great communications and interpersonal skills". I see this time and time again. And the first question I ask myself, is what does this mean? **Be specific.**

Additional Resume Tips and Applying for Project Manager Jobs

For example, are you great at written communication, presenting to large audiences, tailoring communication messaging to key stakeholder groups, meeting planning and facilitation, active listening, etc.? And for interpersonal skills, does this mean you're skilled at negotiation, relationship-building, coaching and mentoring, building trust, etc.?

When writing your resume, **specificity** is critical when you want to set yourself apart. Talk about what specific skills you bring to the table.

Also remember this, your resume is no time to be shy, or lack confidence in your abilities. Communicate your skills and strengths clearly and confidently. Remember, it's not bragging if it's true.

One tip that I want to offer is around comparing your resume to a job posting. *I need to stress this...* Far too many times, project managers look at job postings and immediately disqualify themselves from applying because they don't check off every box listed in the description. You might be doing yourself a huge disservice by deciding to not apply for the opportunity.

Here's the problem, most job postings are written by Human Resource departments, and they often list a long set of qualifications that quite frankly no one can fill. If you think you meet **at least 60% of the requirements listed,** then take the time to apply. The worst-case scenario is you don't get a call. And if that's the case, simply move on.

Also remember this, you probably have similar project management education to many others that have applied. So, use your unique, well-crafted resume to get your foot in the door for an interview. And then you can both assess if you are the *"right fit"* for their team. Remember that it's your skills and your personal brand that set you apart. I've seen in some cases where someone with less experience was hired over someone with more experienced because they were seen as a better fit with the culture of the department and the organization.

Preparing For Your
Project Management Interview

if you get contacted for an interview after submitting your resume, congratulations! You've already passed the first round. They read your resume, you stood out from the crowd, and now they want to learn more about you.

I want you to think about interviews as a **two-way street**. Just as much as they are assessing you to see if you are a good fit for their team, you should also be assessing them to see if they'll provide you with the work environment you're looking for. Remember when we considered what your ideal work environment would look like in an earlier module? You should prepare some questions in advance to better understand their environment, their culture, and any expectations they have for their team. Again, you want to make sure that they'll be a good fit for you as well.

When you're preparing for an interview, make sure you spend some time upfront to research what has been happening in that organization as well as any overall, industry trends. Check to see if they have any recent press releases or updates in the news. You can search for them online, and check out their social media pages. Always have some understanding of what's happening within that organization before the interview occurs.

In advance of the interview, start writing out your answers to some of the most commonly asked questions that nearly every project management interview includes. This way, you already had the opportunity to think through these questions and **master your message**. You can start to create your answers in the worksheets on the next few page. Pre-think scenarios for each of your projects so if a question comes up that address any of these, you've already developed solid examples of what happened, how you addressed it, and what was the outcome and result.

Supercharge Your Project Management Career
Common Interview Questions Worksheet

Develop your answers for how you would respond to these common interview questions.

Tell us about yourself.

Why are you interested in this position / Why do you want this job?

Why are you the best candidate / Why should we hire you?

Why are you planning to leave your current role?

Supercharge Your Project Management Career
Common Interview Questions Worksheet

Develop your answers for how you would respond to these common interview questions.

What is your
ideal work
environment?

What would you
say are your
greatest strengths
and weaknesses?

What would
your current
boss/team say
about you?

What
questions do
you have for
us?

Common Interview Questions Worksheet

Develop your answers for how you would respond to these common interview questions.

Tell us about a time when you had to deal with someone challenging on your project team. What happened and how did you handle it?

Tell us about a time when your project had scope creep. What was the situation and what did you do?

Tell us about a time when a major risk to a project occurred. What happened and how did you mitigate the risk?

Supercharge Your Project Management Career
Common Interview Questions Worksheet

Develop your answers for how you would respond to these common interview questions.

Tell us about a time when you disagreed with a decision that was made. Why did you disagree, and how did you handle the situation?

Tell us about a time when a project went well over time or budget. What happened and what did you do?

Tell us about a time when you had a conflict within the project team. How did you manage the situation and what was the result?

Considerations for During Your Interview

Always have a notepad and pen when you participate in an interview. You should be capturing a few notes especially the names of the interviewers, and any important details they share with you about the role. You should also have any pre-developed questions that you want to ask them written down in advance.

One thing that I've found when I'm interviewing project managers is that few candidates take the time to remember the names of those interviewing them, and actually use their names during the interview. For those that do, they immediately stand out as being personable and engaging. Interviews are meant to be a **two-way conversation**. Make them feel like you're engaged. This will give you bonus points during the interview.

It's also important that when you come to an interview, that you are upbeat, passionate, and excited to be there. You should convey this not just with what you say, but also with your body language. In every way you communicate, you should also demonstrate self-confidence in your abilities. Make them feel just as confident about you so that you stand out from the rest.

Project managers are so used to thinking about what we do in collaboration with our project teams. What ends up happening is that in many interviews I hear candidates say things like "we did this" or "we accomplished that".   Did you pick up on the issue? When you're in an interview, you need to **own the tasks and accomplishments** by saying "I did this" and "I accomplished that". Change your mindset when you are being interviewed, because it's no longer about the team. Instead, it's all about what YOU bring to the table.

If you feel like you mess up on some of the questions, it's ok...here's a little secret...everyone does. Stay calm and don't let that throw you off your game. They'll actually want to see how quickly you recover from a stumble. The faster you brush it off and keep moving, the better.

Thank your interviewers for spending this time with you, and again, use their names when thanking them. Leave them with a great impression, and then follow it up with a thank you email to reiterate your interest and excitement about the role.

Wrap Up and Thank You

Now that you completed the self-assessment, guide, and workbook called Supercharge Your Project Management Career, you are now in a position to set yourself up for success around taking charge of your project management career path.

Thank you for allowing me to be a part of your journey, and I invite you to connect with me on LinkedIn.
You can find me at: **www.linkedin.com/in/natalieberkiwscenna**

Also, if you enjoyed this book and found the information helpful, your 5⭐ review where you purchased this book would be incredibly appreciated - thank you!

Wishing you a ton of success in your project management future!

All my best,
Natalie

Personal Notes

Personal Notes

Personal Notes

Manufactured by Amazon.ca
Bolton, ON

31081386R00033